Published by: Boulder Press, P.O. Box 1583, Solana Beach, Ca 92075
Photography and Text © 2011 Mike Barton

Individual prints may be purchased directly from the photographer: cell phone 720 934-4322
Photographer's website: www.mikebartonphoto.com

Editors: David L. Miles and Ruth Shilling

Library of Congress Control Number: 2010913413
ISBN 13: 978-0-9801024-4-4
ISBN 10: 0-9801024-4-8
Second Edition 2012
Printed in China

Carmel's
Fairy Tale Cottages

photography and text by Mike Barton

BOULDER PRESS

A Great Place is a home and garden shop located in a building built in 1929 by Hugh Comstock

The first time you visit Carmel, you may think you made a wrong turn into Disneyland.

INTRODUCTION

Carmel-by-the-Sea is nestled among sloping forests above a rugged cypress-covered coastline. The charming village is renowned for its magical seaside location with a quaint mixture of art galleries, boutiques, historic inns, cafes and whimsical cottages, all surrounded by breathtaking scenery.

Since everything is within walking distance, it's easy to explore the one square-mile misty village, filled with the scent of eucalyptus, piney woods and jasmine and the sound of waves crashing on the rocky shore. Neighborhoods seem to disappear into the trees and behind foliage along the cozy streets.

James Franklin Devendorf and Frank Powers of San Francisco purchased most of the land in 1900 with a vision to create a haven for intellectuals and eccentrics. They quickly attracted many famous artists, poets and writers such as Robert Lewis Stevenson, Jack London, Robinson Jeffers, Mary Austin, George Sterling, Sinclair Lewis, and Upton

Sinclair. Ansel Adams and Edward Weston lived in the Carmel area where together they took black and white photography to another level.

Later, Carmel became a destination for celebrities. Bing Crosby teamed up with Bob Hope to form the famous "Clam Bake," a winter golf pro-am on Pebble Beach and Cypress Point. Clint Eastwood first came to Carmel on his honeymoon in the 1950s and has lived in the area ever since. He served as mayor of Carmel from 1986-88.

You may notice that there are no parking meters or stoplights in Carmel. And homes still do not have addresses but are instead known by name such as the "Doll House" or "Hansel." Residents need to go to the post office to pick up their mail.

Storybook-style homes became popular in America during the early 1920s and Carmel was no exception. Carmel is home to almost every architectural style ever imagined. You'll discover a unique blend of English storybook cottages, wind-swept roof beach houses, log cabins, rustic redwood cottages, modern all-glass homes and seaside stone castles.

Shortly after moving to Carmel in 1924, Hugh Comstock began to build whimsical cottages that are tucked into different neighborhoods around town. Many other builders began to follow Comstock's lead that furthered the town's storybook ambiance. Locals responded by dressing up their cottages with colorful flowers, and businesses turned barren courtyards into magical gardens that helped to gradually transform Carmel into a full-scale Disneyland.

Carmel makes a perfect launching point for exploring the surrounding forests and spectacular rugged coastline. Or, you may chose to head inland to the many wineries in the valley.

OPPOSITE PAGE AND BELOW: Located down a narrow alleyway is the hidden oasis of the legendary Hog´s Breath Inn made famous by Clint Eastwood. As you enjoy a Dirty Harry cheeseburger, you can feel Eastwood's presence in the larger-than-life photos that surround you.

RIGHT: The 1771 Carmel Mission is home to the first library in California.

MOUNTAINSONG GALLERIES
CARMEL - BY - THE - SEA

CARMEL BAY
COMPANY

Carmel
Dairy

KRIS KRINGLE
of CARMEL

OYSTER BAR
W. SHUCKS
COCKTAILS
LUNCH   DINNER

ABOVE: A surfer's day on Carmel Bay with Pebble Beach Golf Links in the background. The tents along the fairway are set up for the 2010 U.S. Open. **OPPOSITE PAGE**: Pre-dawn along the Big Sur coastline.

OPPOSITE PAGE: This is just a sample of the different styles of cottages found all around Carmel-by-the-Sea.

RIGHT AND BELOW: Many of the fairy tale houses are found on quiet streets like these.

CARMEL-BY-THE-SEA FIRE STATION

OPPOSITE PAGE: Whimsical storefronts quickly followed the theme set by the storybook cottages.

ABOVE: The Carmel Fire Station was built in 1930.

RIGHT: The portholes came from the *Aurora*, an old schooner that went aground in 1935 in Monterey.

PAGES 18-19: Neighborhood streets are dotted with quirky fences, colorful gardens and charming entryways.

OPPOSITE PAGE AND RIGHT: Two of many images along a ribbon of Highway 1 near Big Sur just south of Carmel.

BELOW: The wind couldn't have been blowing any stronger on this evening along Pfeiffer Beach. This is a great place to watch waves crash into rugged shoreline and enjoy spectacular sunsets.

ABOVE: The Bixby Creek Bridge leading to Big Sur was completed in 1931.

OPPOSITE PAGE: The scenic coast along Pacific Grove is located only a few minutes from Carmel between Monterey and Pebble Beach.

LEFT: Dusk along the craggy Monterey coastline.

BELOW: A whale tail is visible far off in the distance after sunset along Asilomar State Beach in Pacific Grove.

OPPOSITE PAGE: The sea stacks along Garrapata Beach are hard to spot from Highway 1. To get this shot, you must climb down a steep, rocky trail to the beach.

ABOVE AND OPPOSITE PAGE: The Edward Kuster house, built in 1920 with granite boulders hauled from the shore below, is nestled in the pines on Carmel Point. Kuster later created the Golden Bough Playhouse.

COTTAGES

Carmel is dotted with fairy tale-style homes thanks to Hugh Comstock. In 1924, he decided to build a tiny cottage for his wife, Mayotta, as a studio for her doll-making hobby as it began to grow into a business. Mayotta rag dolls, called "Otsy-Totsy" dolls, became quite popular during that time.

Comstock built dozens of charming homes around Carmel that make you believe you have stepped into a make-believe world. He bought the lots extremely cheap and built the cottages without great expense. Now, some of these homes are worth millions.

Comstock was neither an architect nor a builder. But he just had the vision to create little whimsical cottages. His storybook design was said to have been inspired by the cottages illustrated by Arthur Rackham in his popular turn-of-the-century children's books. Today, twenty-one of Comstock's original cottages remain in Carmel.

His signature style included steeply pitched and pointy roofs, arched doors and windows, rolled eaves and elfin stone chimneys. This style quickly caught on and nearly thirty storybook-style cottages with a mixture of whimsy and fantasy sprouted up by the late 1920s. Around the same time, architect Robert Stanton and builder M.J. Murphy were developing their own artistic architectural impressions in Carmel.

Many storefronts were redesigned with sweeping roofs, asymmetrical shingles, turrets and stone chimneys as if there was no such thing as a straight line.

Carmel has zoned many of these historical homes to conserve their heritage and now requires approval before remodeling. Take some time and stroll along the quiet streets and admire the many fantasy cottages.

ABOVE: Architect Robert Stanton built the French country-style Normandy Inn in 1924. The half-timbered and staggered shake-roofed Inn is located on Ocean Avenue just up the street from the beach.
OPPOSITE PAGE TOP RIGHT: The office designed and used by Stanton.

OPPOSITE PAGE: The fanciful-looking ticket windows behind the Cottage of Sweets were used by local theatres until 1935.

ABOVE: This 1925 Tudor-style design by Lee Gottfried is home to the PortaBella restaurant.

RIGHT: Casanova makes you feel as if someone plucked it from a small village in Italy or France. The restaurant is as charming and colorful inside as it is outside.

OPPOSITE PAGE TOP: The unusual and imaginative stone cabin named "The Ship" was built in the late 1930s from material salvaged from over fifty ships.

"Sunwisenturn" is a Comstock design completed in 1929. The hard-to-find cottage sits on an irregularly shaped mound under a canopy of trees. Although it is not an exact match, this cottage is the twin to "Our House" shown on on the lower left of page 56.

ABOVE: This little toy cottage is about the size of a toaster.

LEFT: The rustic redwood bark-clad "Bark House" was built in 1922.

OPPOSITE PAGE: Tucked above the shore of Carmel Bay is the Walker House designed by Frank Lloyd Wright. The glass exterior reminds one of a captain's bridge and the wedge-shaped rock wall looks like a ship's hull heading out to sea.

OPPOSITE PAGE: This home sits high on rugged outcroppings directly above the sea.

ABOVE LEFT: In 1928, Hugh Comstock built the charming "Yellow Bird" cottage.

ABOVE RIGHT: This cottage, also shown at the bottom of page 62, seems to blend perfectly with its natural surroundings.

RIGHT: The Hermes House was built by Frederick Bigland after he came from England in the early 1920s.

ABOVE: The Cottage of Sweets features a delicious collection of fudge, locally made chocolates and other sweets. The quaint little English cottage was built on Delores Street in 1922 and rolled down Ocean Avenue on logs the next year to its current location. Since then it has served as a weaving shop, a ticket booth for nearby theatres, a dress shop and finally a candy store in 1960.

LEFT AND OPPOSITE PAGE: The delightful Tea Rose Collection building, complete with mini turrets, is the most unique and colorful building on Ocean Avenue. Architect Michael Murphy designed the building for Edward Kuster based on illustrations from a Swedish folk tale book

ABOVE: Comstock built the "Gretel" cottage in 1925 and tucked it under twisting pines next to "Hansel."

LEFT: "Fables" (1928) is another Comstock cottage nestled among twisted oaks.

OPPOSITE PAGE: The "Windamere" cottage features a multi-level sea wave roof that adds to its rambling look. The hand-crafted shingles with rolled eaves are intended to emulate a thatch roof and give a whimsical character.

ABOVE AND OPPOSITE PAGE: Hugh Comstock's studio built in 1927 later became his wife's residence.

OPPOSITE PAGE: Another whimsical Comstock design, built in 1929.

CLOCKWISE: The half-timbered DeYoe building (1924) built by Michael J. Murphy, the 1926 Bonham house designed by George Mark Whitcomb and Comstock's "Obers" cottage (1925).

LEFT AND BELOW: Poet Robinson Jeffers built the Hawk Tower next to the Tor House, the family residence, as a retreat for his wife and children. After the granite boulders were hauled up from the nearby beach, Jeffers rolled them up a ramp to build the tower.

OPPOSITE PAGE: The T.J. Brennan house was built with native Carmel stone in 1925.

PAGE 56 TOP: The Edward Kuster house sits high on Carmel Point overlooking the sea. Builder Lee Gottfried completed the massive stone house in 1920.

PAGE 56 BOTTOM LEFT: Comstock's "Our House" built in 1928.

PAGE 57: One of the many charming building on Carmel Mission Ranch.

This C.S. Greene design, completed in 1922, sits high on a bluff as waves crash into the rocks below.

ABOVE: Comstock's "Yellowbird" cottage (left) and the hard to photograph 1928 "Dollhouse" (right).

OPPOSITE PAGE TOP: The "Marchen House," built in 1928, is one of Comstock's larger fairy tale cottages.

OPPOSITE PAGE BOTTOM: "Curtain Call," built by Comstock in 1929, is tucked back into a wooded forest.

DOORS AND WINDOWS

The attention to detail may not be more evident than when it comes to doors and windows. Much of the unique handiwork is not always apparent until viewed up close.

Round-topped plank doors with oversized hinges add a medieval flavor to some cottages. Voussoirs of brick and Carmel stone over the archways draw the eye in.

Leaded glass windows and doors with beveled glass panes are common, and charming arched windows are a popular choice. An array of cast and wrought-iron outdoor lighting fixtures add a decorative flair to entrances.

Hugh Comstock's business sign still hangs outside his former office. Carmel chalk stone forms the arched door and helps the transition to the stucco exterior.

ABOVE CLOCKWISE: The T.J. Brennan House, "Windamere" cottage, the Stone House and "Hanel."

Allen Knight collected
nautical artifacts and
used parts from over
fifty ships to build
a stone ship cabin
named "The Ship."
The wood planks and
portholes came from
the *Aurora*, a four-
masted schooner
that grounded on
Monterey Beach durir
a storm in 1935. The
red door is from the
USS Farquhar (DD-
304), a Navy destroye
commissioned in 192

CHIMNEYS AND FIREPLACES

Unusual elfin chimneys and fireplaces are often favorite subjects for the whimsical imagination. They come in all sizes with sloped or stepped profiles.

Many of the cottages have at least one fireplace. Hugh Comstock designed his fireplaces so that they would disappear into a high vaulted ceiling.

OPPOSITE PAGE: A broad Carmel stone chimney dominates the south side of "Sunwiseturn." The facade is similar to its twin, "Our House," on page 56.

BELOW LEFT: This stand-alone fireplace sits far back in someone's front yard.

BELOW RIGHT: Completed in 1926, this cottage was originally an art studio.

ABOVE AND PAGE 78: The two stone fireplaces in the Hog's Breath Inn dining room

OPPOSITE PAGE CLOCKWISE: The charming children's boutique Kids by The Sea, one of many fire pits in the Hog's Breath Inn courtyard, another Comstock fireplace and a look inside the Tuck Box

ABOVE AND PAGES 88-89: Some of Comstock's many whimsical fireplaces made of Carmel chalk stone.

Y ARDS AND F ENCES

Cottage owners take great pride in their homes and act like caretakers. The results can be seen inside and out.

Lush gardens and attractive landscaping surround many of these storybook creations and help them blend into their natural environment.

Fences come to life with an abundant array of vibrant flowers and foliage. Some of the wooden pickets are intentionally misaligned to give a cartoonish look or the impression that the fence is very old.

Carmel is full of many colorful courtyards. Some are right off the main streets, while others are left to stumble upon when exploring quiet alleyways.

My
Garden
Was in full
Bloom last Week
Sorry You
missed it!

LEFT AND BELOW: The twenty-two acre Carmel Mission Ranch, located on the south end of Carmel, was restored by longtime Carmel resident Clint Eastwood. The former dairy farm was going to be turned into a condo development until Eastwood purchased the property and made it into a charming resort.

ABOVE AND OPPOSITE PAGE TOP: A Michael Murphy design near the ocean.
OPPOSITE PAGE BOTTOM: The impeccably landscaped grounds of the La Playa Hotel.

ENTRYWAYS AND CAR PARKS

Many of the storybook homes have well-groomed pathways leading up to front doors that look like scenes from the "Wizard of Oz." The staggered brick walkways beg for a visit, while ivy and flower-draped arbors seem to invite you in.

Tiny toylike garages seem to need a shoehorn to help slide in the vehicle.

A Great Place, located behind the Tuck Box, is a fun place in which to browse.

A look Inside

Many of the cottages have small kitchens, dining rooms and bathrooms with low ceilings, as if they were designed for elves.

Their inadequate size has required many past and present owners to renovate to make them more roomy and useful. Some have painstakingly preserved their cottages to maintain their historical character.

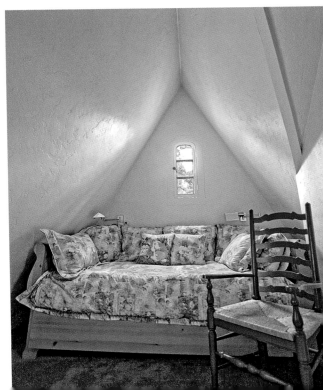

OTHER BOOKS BY MIKE BARTON

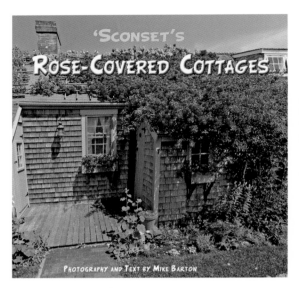

THANKS

Many thanks to all the homeowners for their patience when I knocked on doors and trampled lawns while taking the photos for this book.

ABOUT THE PHOTOGRAPHER

Mike Barton is a photographer from Solana Beach, California. A native of Michigan, Mike moved to sunny California after graduating from Michigan State. Michigan is a great place to "be from."

Photography became a true passion when he moved to Boulder, Colorado where he tried to photograph every square inch of the Colorado mountains.

While living still in Boulder, Mike ventured back to California in 2010 to capture the charming neighborhoods of Carmel-by-the-Sea. He returned in 2013 to take photos for this second edition.

People often comment on the vibrant colors that Mike is able to bring out in his photographs. This requires returning to the same place over and over until the light and other conditions are just right. A photo can be taken of the same location on different days and the clouds, colors, waves and reflections can vary dramatically.

Mike began a children's book series titled "The Adventures of Magic" in 2014. There are now five books in the series.

To see more of Mike's work, please visit his website: www.mikebartonphoto.com.